Adjust Your Set

Adjust Your Set

Linda Stitt

Le Conseil des Arts
du Canada
DEPUIS 1957

The Canada Council
for the Arts
SINCE 1957

NATURAL HERITAGE BOOKS

Adjust Your Set
Linda Stitt

Published by Natural Heritage / Natural History Inc.,
P.O. Box 95, Postal Station O,
Toronto, Ontario, M4A 2M8

Cover Design Blanche Hamil, Norton Hamil Design
Text Production, Morley Chalmers
in Adobe Garamond, using QuarkXPress on a Macintosh Quadra 950.
Printed and bound in Canada on recycled acid-free paper by Hignell Printing Limited,
Winnipeg, Manitoba.

Canadian Cataloguing in Publication Data

Stitt, Linda, 1932 —
Adjust your set

Poems.
ISBN 1-896219-32-2

I. Title.

PS8587.T58A84 1997   C811'.54   C97-931438-0
PR9199.3.S74A84 1997

Le Conseil des Arts   The Canada Council
du Canada   for the arts
Depuis 1957   since 1957

Natural Heritage / Natural History Inc. gratefully acknowledges the support received for its
publishing program from the Canada Council Block Grant program. We also acknowledge
with gratitude the assistance of The Association for the Export of Canadian Books, Ottawa.

Dedication

This book is dedicated to the memory of Kema Ananda, my beloved brother and teacher, whose life and death were joyous expressions of the dharma, and to his wife, Woon, who, out of her infinite compassion, continues the great work.

It is dedicated, also, to the spirit of my mother, still teaching me by revered example.

A few of these poems were previously published in "Uncritical Mass in Consort", a collection privately compiled and published with my two partners, Cecilie Kwiat and Charlene D. Jones, — to whom I publicly express limitless love and gratitude for their affection and support.

The balance of the poems were selected from a glut of new work, with the aid of my dear and dedicated friends, Sita Holland, Joanne Bersudsky, and Syd Pettit—(don't blame me, blame them). I can't adequately thank them for their time, effort and honesty.

Dharma Dorje and Punnadhammo Bhikkhu shared their insight and understanding with me on many occasions, and I am truly grateful.

Morley Chalmers, my dear and dependable chum has, once again, donated his astute and efficient labours in typesetting and design. Much obliged, Morley.

And I thankfully acknowledge the contributions of my children, Paula and Kim Stitt, who have been unfailingly patient, generous, helpful, reliable and irreverent and have never once threatened to change their names.

And, finally, I owe my profound appreciation to Barry, Jane and Nancy Penhale, and Heather Wakeling, my publishers, editors and friends, for their confidence, encouragement and expertise.

"If Stitt decided which voice she preferred, she could write credible devotional poetry, snappy eipgrams, humorous children's poetry, or solid free verse; mashed into the same volume, however, the collection demands too much aesthetic adjustment from the reader."

From Canadian Book Review Annual, 1992
— reviewing **Insights and Outlooks**.

In honour of a number of my readers who have assured me that they are quite capable of, and even amused by, following my meanderings, this book is respectfully titled **Adjust Your Set**.

Table of Contents

New wrinkle — Old fool

I love these wrinkles around my eyes,

    they make me look wise.

        — It's a disguise.

My new literacy

Last month, my son, in an excess of filial benevolence, delivered to me his old computer, having satisfactorily upgraded himself to a status which I assume to be comparable to Science Officer of the Starship Enterprise.

You may deduce that I am confused, denigrated and intimidated by technology. But you must also be made aware that my son is bigger, younger, smarter and far more self assured than I, and I have not yet totally shed, in my liberated antiquity, a loathsome tendency to accede, dutifully and unquestioningly, to masculine domination. This is a filthy habit, to which I confess reluntantly, but it explains why I rarely reject that which my male offspring has decided, in his wisdom, is for my own good. In other words, I am conditioned to accept his gratuitous stallion without examining the state of its dentition.

This gift horse, however, carries about it a pungent whiff of the Trojan. Nothing safe about it. Having successfully infiltrated the sanctum sanctorum of my office cum garret, necessitating the redeployment of my Babels of papers from six towers into half that number, — but higher, it sits, in equine innocence, ready to disgorge more ills than Pandora's box.

I sit before the keyboard, communing with esoteric terms like bytes and format and function and alt. My palms sweat, my fingers tremble. I am about to unleash a power with a potential more dangerous than Zeus's thunderbolts. One blunder will let fly the forces of annihilation. One thoughtless slip, one skid of an unwary finger and the juggernaut will be loosed. The screen will explode into smoking fragments of glass and metal. My floor will tremble and the walls of my building will fall in upon me. The structure will collapse, shaking apart the streets and edifices of this city block. The metropolis will shudder and crash into its substructure, knocking the continent from its underpinnings. Tectonic plates will be hurled apart and volcanoes, earthquakes, tsunamis and whirlwinds will wreak devastation. The cataclysm will be joined. The stars will go out. Judgement Day will be upon us.

This is not, for me, the stuff of poetry. That to which computers inspire me is most certainly the fabric of prose. And that is why this poem sounds more like an essay.

Ancient wisdom

Here's sixty-three years of wisdom revealed
in a statement succinct and terse, —
    Life doesn't get any better than this.
    Just be glad if it doesn't get worse.

Summing up at sixty

Give me a moment and lend me your ears
and I'll tell you what I've learned in three score years.

Exercise. Take care of your eyes.
Close your mouth when you're swatting flies.
    Meditate, and stand up straight;
    sleep in the morning if you stay out late.
Enjoy your youth; tell the truth;
chocolate's the best cure for a sweet truth.
    Retreat in order to advance.
    Dance every dance and laugh every chance;
    guffaw and giggle and chortle and chuckle.
    Don't get caught under anyone's knuckle.
Show respect and don't neglect
to be polite and circumspect
but never let it hold you back
when it's time to tell 'em "Fuck you, Jack."
    Learn generosity; avoid pomposity;
    smile without malice at animosity.
Endeavor to give as well as you take.
Don't swim where the sewer goes into the lake.
    Don't be fidgety, don't be jumpy.
    Don't be dismayed when your body gets lumpy.
Don't hold a grudge. Try not to judge.
Look out for the shells in pistachio fudge.
    Don't be a whiner and don't be a boaster.
    Don't stick the butter knife in the toaster.
Bullshit doesn't help your garden grow;
try saying you're sorry but you just don't know.
    No one's at fault and no one's to blame
    but men and women are not the same.
Of course, it's always your decision
but you don't have to buy someone else's vision.
    Don't grab and claw and cling and clutch.
    When you know too little, don't say too much.

Question the word of sinner and saint
but believe the signs that say "Wet Paint."
Speak your mind and say your piece.
Don't roll in the sand when you're covered with grease.

If there's something here that you can use,
feel free to take it, should you choose,
provided that we first agree
these lessons are lessons from me to me,
for the greatest lesson, a word to the wise,
is it's not advisable to advise.

The matricide

I was not her firstborn,
not her only child,
but by some mishap of my birth,
some changeling rage,
some malevolent mutation,
I have wandered from my mother's line
and made a family of my desires.

My pleasure was my power.
I created a god who gave me dominion
and took my mother for my slave,
my wet nurse and my concubine.

I have bound her with fetters
ripped from her sinews
and throttled her with a garrote
fashioned from her own stripped veins.

I have blinded her with acid
and fouled her tears
with my excrement.
I wear her teeth as bracelets
and smear my face
with the secretions of her glands.
I have torn out her hair
and plucked the down from her limbs
to adorn myself in savage splendour.

I have committed conflagrations,
infernos, holocausts
upon her skin
and paid no heed to her convulsions.
I have poured greed and hatred
and holy wars
down her throat
and masturbated against her thighs
as she shuddered, writhed,
and vomited molten agony.

I have shattered her eardrums
and stolen her voice
with noxious thunder;
poisoned her exhalations
of sweet grass, cedar, sage
and uncorrupted smoke
with mephitic fulminations of debauchery.
I have sucked dry her bountiful teats,
which withheld nothing and, unsatisfied,
sunk my ravening fangs into her breast
and gorged myself upon her blood.

I have flattened her mounds with merciless blows
and filled her crevices with degradation.
I have pierced her organs
and gulped her juices
and cannibalized my siblings
who sought a gentler share.

I have saddened her and shamed her,
degraded and debauched her
and yet she loved me
and cradled me in her vast generosity
even as she died.
And now I lie shivering
against her cold, bruised belly,
pinching and kneading and clawing
the moribund flesh
and shrieking,
in slack-jawed, uncomprehending terror,
"More. More. Give me more."

Artifact

I was offered a paint-by-the-numbers life
of circumscribed colours and designs,
with traditional patterns, nice and neat,
but I couldn't stay within the lines.

So I scribbled outside my social class,
my duties as mother and as wife,
and I scrawled my name on experience.
It may not be art, but it's my life.

And often it stirs me into the crowd
and sometimes it sets me far apart.
It spatters my senses with splashes of bliss
and dashes love's pigments into my heart
and I am quite content with this
untidy life, my artless art.

For heaven's sake

For the love of me,
I can do little
to ease the suffering
of this world,
grown harsh and brittle.
But,
knowing that all life is one,
interdependent,
I strive with diligence
toward the mind transcendent.
For the love of all,
I take this aspiration,
I will stand helpless
in the face of pain
and seek purification.
And this is all,
for the love of me,
for the love of you,
with the greatest compassion,
I can do.

As I live and learn

Mean average

My excesses and asceticisms
fling me far and wide
and the middle path consists, for me,
of careening from side to side.

Form vs function

Some of us get ourselves enmeshed
in religious trappings;
others have managed to keep the gift
and discard the wrappings.

Sweet grapes

The less I possess, the freer I'll be.
I've said it before and I mean it,
for if I don't own it, I'm sure you'll agree,
I probably won't have to clean it.

Grist

It caught my eye ...
    a falling leaf?
        a wounded bird?
I caught my breath in comprehension,
    begging disbelief,
for, as it stirred,
I saw a tiny sparrow
    huddled on the pavement
and, in the single brief
and prudent moment
    that I did not dare
    to brave the ruthless traffic,
it was too late;
    caution became the thief
    of my compassion
and, to my cowardly shame,
there was nothing left to do
but bid my spirit
lift that guttered spark
to the eternal flame
    and all my day was touched
    with impotence
    and guilt and grief.

And yet, you see,
in spite of all the proper words I've said,
I did not hesitate to grind those fragile bones
to make my bread.

I am always with you, he said

Deep within the now,
the honey nectar
of the moment present,
is freedom.

The universe
    peeks at me around a crinkled corner,
    squints at me from a dusty sunbeam,
    winks at me in a diamond ice drop,
    beckons me from a mirrored window,
    opens its infinitely petalled flower,
presents itself
in countless aspects.

How could one,
    dancing in totality,
be fettered by desire?
Nothing is absent,
nothing is omitted,
nothing is excluded.

In each particle
of the all,
all is.

City garden

I grow peppermint for my morning tea
and aloe to soothe my skin,
parsley to decorate my plate
and cleanse my garlicky grin.
I grow basil for my sauces, —
I'll give you some for yours,
and lavender for fat sachets
to scent my dresser drawers.
I grow savory and marjoram
to flavour my vegetable stews
and lots of chives, that I can find
a dozen ways to use.
I grow sorrel for my salads,
there's bite in every bowl,
and I grow sweet grass and sage
for just the joy of my soul.

Mindless

A skein of geese
weaves itself through twilight
with a perfection
so awesome
and so grand
that I am
for a blissful, silent moment
freed from my compulsion
to name,
to count,
to understand.

The old grey mare

Self-discipline
comes easy to me now.

Of course
one rarely has to rein in
a dead horse.

My passions now
are seldom,
few
and, mostly, purified.
They have no need to be denied.
I mount them
as my chariots of bliss
and ride.

Nada, nil, niente, zero, zip, zilch

I am nothing if not resilient.
I bob and bend and dance
to the currents of luck and chance
and the inconsistent winds of circumstance.

I am nothing if not flexible.
Whatever may befall, I can adjust,
I must
honour that primal order I profess to trust.

I am nothing if not self reliant,
splendidly defiant
against adversity, a veritable giant.

But I am nothing if not naked and empty
at your leaving,
grieving,
bereft of all believing,
fate's uncomprehending toy.
My small attempts at courage,
spontaneity and joy
were all about you
and without you
I am nothing.

Well, maybe not nothing, —
more like a stolid mass of self pity,
void of direction,
incapable of movement.
Nothing
would be an improvement.

Roses

I do not open up my senses
in the city,
I have forgotten how to trust.
Betrayed too often
by cacophony and dust,
I tend to wall myself in quasi-catatonic inner carping,
more's the pity.

But spare the pity,
I have friends of great compassion
who know me well
and will not let me fashion
of my retreat a cell
— rather a peaceful, permeable citadel.

And so they come and gather me
before my mortar hardens
and take me to a lakeside park
to walk among the fountains
and the flower gardens
and they laugh and smile and nod their heads,
empowering me to walk into the rich, prolific beds
where a delight of smell and sight discloses
roses,
roses, roses, only roses.

Roses jovial and merry,
gregarious and solitary;
roses riotous and raucous
in seclusion and in caucus;
blowsy, frowsy roses,
roses without shame
who make no secret of their sensuality
and celebrate their transitory fame.

Roses courageous,
standing undaunted as each petal falls;
roses that should be painted on black velvet
and hung on brothel walls;
roses that are a put-on of perfection,
dreaming in self-centred introspection;
gentle roses, wicked roses, innocent roses;
roses of generosity and soul so great
I want to jump right in and pollinate;
roses of shyness, roses of valour,
roses suffused, roses of pallor;
roses of carnal undertones
and satin overlay;
roses as spare as desert bones,
roses as lush as Valentine's Day;
roses virginal, serene, angelic;
day-glo roses, neon, psychedelic.

A pot-pourri of roses,
each of them doing its part,
giving the best of its fragrance
out of its occult heart,
breathing raspberry whispers,
sighing cinnamon sighs;
revelations of roses
are redolent and wise;
roses gracious, ostentatious,
bumptious, sumptuous, salacious;
roses fervid and assertive;
roses coy but never furtive;
roses effusive, roses reclusive,
roses plebian, roses exclusive;
roses insolent and modest.

The most common and the oddest
bring delight and wonder to this place
and restore me to a state of grace.

And, with my faith renewed by roses,
I dare, with careless and unwary daring,
to open, once again, my ears,
here, by a tranquil meditation pond.
And when it hears,
in a naked and unguarded moment,
a finch's song,
trilling compellingly above
the drone of traffic,
the mind rebels at such simplicity,
leaps into silence,
falls into love.

Woman in question

I never questioned that fathers knew best,
that husbands were always obeyed,
that God was a man who required that His children
be dutiful, meek and afraid.
I never questioned that women must be
docile and nubile, lovely and slender
and grateful for masculine time and attention
given the female, inferior gender.

I never questioned till almost too late,
till shame was too solid
and hope too ethereal,
till father was dead
and husband divorced
and duty dissolved
and God immaterial.

Laundry list

Do not think
    these are the sheets
    he slept between,
    this is the pillowcase
    on which he laid his head.
Consider only
    lifting
    shaking
    stretching
    spreading
    smoothing out
                  instead.

And, if the mind
slips into fantasy,
give it a prompt and gentle scolding
and go on marking folding
and unfolding.

Mad about you

Anger smolders and swirls in me,
kindling emotion into incandescence.
I am an oven, a cauldron, a volcano.
The rivers of my body seethe with wrath,
my exhalations consume forests.
My senses are ablaze in choler;
oceans boil at my glance;
my touch melts mountains.
I scorch the skies with flares of fury,
withering clouds and shrivelling sunlight.
My tongues of flame lick flesh into cinders.
Seething and spitting,
hissing and snarling,
I am a furnace of rage,
an inferno of ire,
an inextinguishable conflagration
and yet
your smallest tear
can quench me.

Last turning

You were the man
who put an end
to the chances I took with men
and the pain of parting was not as great
as the pain of seeing you again,
  the pain of feeling
  the moon tides of emotion
  weaving wanting back into the pattern
  of my days,
    regretting circumstance
    which drove the currents of our drifting
    separate ways,
      resenting ebbs and flows
      which cast us up on different beaches,
            things as they are,
            which order me to the far reaches
            of your life.
And I could apprehend a future
rife with misery
if it were not for love,
reminding me,
in spite of all we had before,
to let the past completely go
and, in the present, know
I never loved you more.

Bone yard

After you leave,
I scavenge through the bones
of our relationship
to see what sustenance remains,
but all my searching yields
little to nourish me,
for all my pains.

The empty shells
of my bereavement
remind me of the shock, denial, anger,
desperation, fear
I hatched in quick succession
at finding our tomorrows
abandoned here.

And I am overwhelmed by grief
until, at last,
I find the letting go,
accepting what must be,
knowing it must be so.

Now, here I sit,
gathering shards and fragments,
patiently and alone,
blunting with equanimity
their painful points and edges,
lovingly
polishing ivory out of bone.

Blocks
and
unblocks

I've been shaking myself up lately,
looking to see what it's all about,
building concepts on top of concepts
                  and pulling the bottom one out.

Getting to know me

Hindsight

The present lesson
        I reject,
I only learn
        in retrospect.

No trespass

I try to remember,
when the going gets hard,
that the universe invited me
to play in its yard.

Capacity for tenacity

When courage couldn't make it
and wisdom wouldn't quite do,
stubborness was all I had left
and stubborness carried me through.

Blue surge

Call it anger,
    it will rage in you.
Call it fear
    and you will tremble.
Call it energy.
    You will see
    the way it can resemble
    the model
    shaped by your experience
    and expectation.
        The power
        loses nothing in translation
so call it love
    and it will light your days,
    illuminate and liberate your years.

As a thing is viewed,
so it appears.

With a little help

My friends
do not allow me
    the indulgence of self-pity
    the arrogance of unworthiness
    the insolence of fear
    the insularity of separateness.

They lead me
    drive me
    harass me
to clearer vision
and broader understanding.

They do not require me to judge
but only to discriminate.

They honour me with compassion
with humour and spontaneity.

I thought I had abandoned
the pursuit of enlightenment
but I am forced to reconsider.
Could it be
that I have chosen the path
of liberation through peer pressure?

Poem for today

Even last month,
if you had turned up at my door
I could have cast the past away
for only that and nothing more.
I would have recklessly ignored
experience's warnings and alarms
for the remembered joy of coming home
to the small circle of your arms.
A month ago,
hope might have washed away the fears
that spread their isolating residue
over my years
and I, perhaps, (oh surely)
would have stepped out of the husks
of pain and pride
into the still communion I once felt
at simply being by your side.
Only last month,
if you had come, by chance,
and found me waiting in the wings
and beckoned me,
I might have dared to dance.
And just your presence
would have spoken all you had to say,
last month,
        last week,
            yesterday.

Some time

Sometimes,
all it takes is time
to fill the canyons of emptiness,
silt up the torrents of loneliness,
dry up the wellspring of regret.
Sometimes,
love takes all joy when it departs,
diverts the stream sustaining thirsty hearts,
steals off with the elixir needed to forget,
empties the source of peace and passion,
breaks the bucket which drew forth
the cure for life's great wounds
and little aches.
Sometimes,
for the fortunate,
time is all it takes.

Time heals

Time has veiled my recollection
of your icy anger
and your fiery scorn
and I confess that,
though I was relieved to leave you,
I am often lonely and forlorn
for only the memory
of your sometimes tenderness
lingers with me,
sweet and fresh.
And you're a far better man
in my mind
than you were
in the flesh.

The authority

I miss it still,
having him to ask
about every question
and any task,

how to wire a plug,
shampoo a rug,
the pros and cons of a Volkswagon bug,

how to build a fire,
how to change a tire,
how to dress a lesion and strip a wire,

where the fish are caught,
how to tie a knot,
how to sit a canter and post a trot,

how to cinch a girth,
help a mare give birth,
a gelding's age and what he's worth,

how to thread a pipe,
how to hunt a snipe,
how to tell if a canteloup is ripe,

where to dig a well,
who has land to sell,
how lintel and sash are built parallel,

how to sharpen a knife,
live a blameless life,
the proper deportment for a wife.

Whatever there was to know, he knew
and he tried to tell me a time or two
the what, the where, the how
but, hell, I didn't listen then
and I probably wouldn't now.

Lady's choice

I will not turn my mind to you tonight
to revisit loneliness and loss,
  that is a land where I no longer dwell.
   The expectation was unreasonable,
   the betrayal was mutual,
   the relief is palpable.
The present is seasonable
and as it should be.
  The past was hell.
I rest my thoughts
on what arises
in the moment,
wishing you farewell
  and well
    and well.

Death, retreat, or a good, long nap

Into the fertile grave I go
with all I am and all I know,
all form and personality,
perception, rationality,
interred in darkness, stirred into
potential, in the cosmic brew.
And, if I cleanly leave behind
the mortal flesh, the narrow mind,
the selfish thought, the partial sight,
the tomb becomes a womb of light.
I see with universal eyes
and, from the fertile grave, I rise.

Liberation

Sing hey, sing ho
for the wrathful gods,
they're always welcome here.
Once
what you most feared
has happened,
there's nothing more to fear.

Ladies' choice

Ladies, don't lose your women friends
when a new love comes to town,
'cause your women friends will lift you up
when your lover lets you down
and your women friends will tell you true
when your lover tells you lies
and when your heart is broken
they'll come by and sympathize.
They'll celebrate your new romance
and cheer you when it ends,
for men folk are just lovers
but women folk are friends.

Fetal vision

Moving through this dark corridor,
conception to consciousness,
struggle is all,
security a lie,
complacency anathema to question.
Refusing to be born,
we die.

There is a season

Trudging through the park,
I begged a blossom of a linden tree
to carry to the bedside
of someone dear to me.

The bloom will wilt;
its scent will dissipate within the hour
and my dear one will not be here
when next the lindens flower.

The castaway

At the residence, the nurses
have been bringing her for years
to my classes, and I welcome her,
but I'm not sure she hears.
She is absent though she's present
and she can't recall her name
and I don't know if she listens
but I say "I'm glad you came.
Please come again next Thursday."
It's rare for her to speak
but she always smiles and whispers,
"I'll be going home next week."

Cecilie

Close your eyes
and cover your faces.
She moves now
through the in-between spaces
where dwells divinity.
She dances in this very moment
with the fulness of infinity,
the emptiness of ego
viewed with uncompromising clarity.
She shapes arisings to the present need
and all with humour and with charity
and with the unrehearsed compassion
that gives completely
without stint or ration,
wherever want is audibly or silently expressed.
Till you can bear to see her dressed
only in virtue,
only in light that burns away all traces
of self-protecting greed,
of self-excusing lies,
cover your faces,
close your eyes.

For Jaredene

Who can I tell about you?
You were the one I told everything to
and even before I could say it, you knew.
Now who can I tell about you?

Friends don't come easy to me.
I know lots of people, but those I feel free
to confide in and open my heart to are few.
So who can I tell about you?

You never did the usual thing.
You opened my eyes and you managed to bring
to every occasion a fresh point of view.
I never could tell about you.

Everything changes and passes away,
sometimes even love is no reason to stay.
We all have to do what we all have to do.
But who can I tell about you?

We shared our joy and we shared our pain
in a symbiosis I can't explain.
We made a oneness out of two
and I don't know how, and I don't know who
I can possibly tell about you.

Birth day

Where she walked
potential blossomed into blessing
like clear refreshing water
filling the footprints
of a passing saint.
We who loved her
drank in her presence,
were nourished by her graciousness
and grace.
She should have died
surrounded by disciples
studying the seamless fluidity
of her realization.
Relinquishing
attachment to position
she moved from glory to glory
and left behind no mourning for identity
but celebration of a task completed,
transcending separation in non-clinging transition,
experiencing totality,
oneness with the mother light.
Her death was a birth into immanence
and a gift of communion.

Homecoming

Take me.
I will go with you
    and leave my duties all behind,
        entrusted to your keeping.
I will leave
    my loves and hates,
        my laughter and my weeping,
my silver bracelets
    and my golden beads
        and all that I possess,
my truths, my lies,
    my poetry.
        Those things I can't express
and those things
    half and still inadequately said
        I leave to your summation
and, naked, come to liberation,
    shedding the last shreds of my separateness,
        growing whole,
bringing back to you my soul.

At a loss

At last,
    after the bittersweet, cathartic eulogy
    and the long procession,
        threaded through indifferent traffic,
we stood
    circling the raw, unresolved grave
    in the marble garden.

Then,
    with the final rites recited,
the women wept
and the men grasped crusted spades
    to render,
        each in turn,
    their ultimate service.

The young men laboured slowly,
    musing on mortality
and the old men shovelled frantically,
    building a levee
    between themselves and death.

Dense clods
drummed loudly upon the coffin lid
    in a dreadful rhythm,
    hollow and strange,
        but chillingly familiar.

    Shivering,
I trolled with memory
    through nightmare and loss,
    through horrors real and imagined
and snagged the sorry recognition
of the stentorian beating
of my own empty heart.

Valediction

    Ashes to summer breezes, Mum,
dust to the wave,
better borne on water and air
than lowered into the grave.
Better delivered from blood and bone
than lie in the dark and rot.
Better remembered for what you are
than what you were not.
Never the spirit crippled,
although the flesh had failed,
no dimming of the consciousness
but mother light unveiled
through loneliness and helplessness,
acceptance of the pain
with dignity and courage.
    Ride on the wind and rain
until the mortal leavings
fly where the past has fled.
Live in the deathless.
    Only
that which could die
is dead.

Father

He grows fragile now,
in my protective memory,
not the puissant giant
I knew him once to be.
I held him lightly,
this gossamer of spirit
freed fom flesh,
this fabric worn from heavy cloth
to flimsy mesh,
this almost flown
from ash of body,
charred remains of bone
given to wave and wind.
I fear the years
will stealthily rescind
the essence that I knew,
as it turns insubstantial,
seeps away,
like rain on thirsty earth.
I must now grasp him tightly
and pay the grief
so great a loss is worth,
feeding my heart
as kindling to his flame,
remembering,
in spite of sorrow and of pain,
the splendour, joy and power
of his name.
I laugh, sometimes,
remembering,
sometimes I cry.
We are not yet finished,
he and I.

Dying wish
A Buddhist perspective on the hereafter

I do not want to go to heaven,
that is not my aspiration.
Heaven, in my understanding,
still turns upon the wheel
of dependent origination
and, though blissful they may be,
though brilliant and sublime,
heavenly states still spin within duality,
governed by impermanence and time.
The gods, however glorious
and mighty in their day,
are subject, over eons,
to downfall and decay.
Heaven, in its splendour
is merely a resting place
along the evolutionary way,
not (thus have I heard) the destination,
just a nice place for a vacation
along the noble path to liberation.
And those who dwell in heavenly forms,
as purified as they may be,
as joyous and compassionate and gentle,
must brave again the pain of human life
to seek cessation in the transcendental.

And I don't want to go to heaven
for, as far as I can tell,
heaven, if one has not attained
to saintly patience,
must be a kind of hell.
But the road has already been devilish hard —
as far as I've gone with it —
so just give me, please, a speedy rebirth,
and let me get on with it.

Conjugating the spectrum

People ask me, on occasion,
where I get my inspiration
and I tell them I invariably find
subjects made for contemplation,
objects born for speculation
as I conjugate the spectrum of my mind.

sunsets and rainbows,
shadows on dust,
essence of moonbeams,
reliance and trust,

fire in the firmament,
sunshine and rain,
wind across ashes,
confusion and pain,

waiting and weariness,
ginger wind blowing,
ageing and weakening,
greening and growing,

courage and cowardice,
villain or hero,
absolute nonsense,
absolute zero,

fern fronds unfurling,
tighly curled fists,
radiant energy,
listlessness, lists,

emerald memories,
amethyst streams,
ruby begonias,
peridot dreams,

silicone valleys,
soft-slipping clay,
dewdrops and vapour,
pain and decay,

freckles and wrinkles,
doubt and disease,
symphonic flavours,
welcome of trees,

sparrows in winter,
narcissus in spring,
summer's wild berries,
autumn's last fling,

choral vibration,
crystal reflection,
life and eternity,
faith and affection,

birth and beginning,
bound to the wheel,
hope for the wicked,
search for the real,

slow fragmentation,
alienation,
instant and total
gratification,

sometime and never,
fiction and learning,
far constellations
turning and turning,

cumulo nimbus,
unending question,
volcanic statement,
jasmine suggestion,

time and its opposite,
plane of duality,
coolness and charity,
work and morality,

bodily wisdom,
mental confusion,
life more abundant,
nature's profusion,

love and compassion,
(seldom and sparse)
comic absurdity,
laughter and farce,

losing and winning,
waiting and when,
death and beginning
over again,

humour and fellowship,
famine and war,
flute in mythology,
after, before,

hopes, aspirations,
aversions and fears,
elements, senses,
seconds and years,

soft-centred chocolates,
soft summer breezes,
soft-hearted cynics,
soft ripened cheeses,

taking directions,
taking the cake,
take it or leave it,
give me a break,

human stupidity,
greed and pollution,
human nobility,
search for solution,

full frontal nudity,
cellular sounds,
poetic obsession,
burial mounds,

past irresponsible,
future a mess,
present uncertain,
joy, nonetheless,

fond recollections
of high times and tokes,
thangkas and tangos
and family jokes,

voice of the universe
oming and humming,
light without limit,
being...
       becoming...

species and specimens
dead and extinct,
oneness of allness,
life interlinked,

tastes of tomorrows
of seeds underground,
texture of odour
of colour of sound,

under suspicion,
over the wall,
mind over matter,
spring above all,

Forewarning

Look away from beauty,
beauty is to fear.
Beauty grabs you by the heart
and hauls you over here.
Beauty grips you by the gut
and hurls you over there;
beauty shatters you to bits
and spreads you everywhere.
Beauty takes you by the throat
and blows your breath away,
she holds you captive in the night
and hostage by the day.
Once you've tasted beauty,
you can never stop;
beauty puts the spurs to you
and rides you till you drop.
Beauty doesn't care a bit
for manners or convention,
she insists on nothing less
than your complete attention.
Beauty steals your mind
and gives you rapture in its place;
beauty casts a spell on you
by showing you her face.
Beauty is the bait
and beauty is the hook.
You'll be seeing beauty
anywhere you look,
above, below and deep within.
Pervading through and through,
beauty's gonna get you.
    Love will, too.

Song of the frigid woman
        or
Baby, it's cold inside

Oh Lord, please give me an impotent man.
I enjoy a good hug whenever I can
but celibacy is my ultimate plan,
so give me an impotent man.

He could be taking some strong medication
that dampens his drive, or have some combination
of injury, age, ennui and castration,
just give me an impotent man.

I haven't completely abandoned romance,
I just choose to relate where there isn't the chance
stepping out might involve stepping out of my pants.
Please give me an impotent man.

No thrill in the masculine member I find
since my worn out libido just up and resigned,
but I love intercourse with the masculine mind,
so give me an impotent man.

The truth must be told and the facts must be faced,
no man in his prime or his senses would waste
a moment in chasing the forcibly chaste,
so give me an impotent man.

Oh Lord, please don't send me some lusty young buck
because I'm convinced, with my usual luck,
I'd want conversation and he'd want to physically
        express his affection.
Oh give me an impotent man.

Outsider

I did not realize
that I am all and all is me
in every aspect
and in each direction,
and I have stood
with my nose against the glass,
envying my own reflection.

Just call it love

I woke up this morning with nothing to say,
no reason to kick off the covers
until I decided this must be the day
for writing a poem just for lovers —

for lovers of every dimension and shape,
of all inclinations and sizes,
whatever our languages, ages or shades,
whatever our masks and disguises,

for those who are awkward and shy about love
and those who are brazen and bold,
for those who came loving into the world
or found love when they had grown old,

for those to whom love is a finite reserve,
laid by for relations and friends
and those who go squandering boundless amounts
from accounts whose supply never ends,

for those to whom love is a burden at times
and those who can carry it lightly,
for those who are ponderous bores about love
and those who are witty and sprightly,

for those to whom love is a place in the soul
where the gifts of the cosmos converge
and those to whom love is a thing of the flesh,
a mere biological urge,

for those who are frozen and icy in love
and others who tremble and burn,
for those to whom love came as simply as breath
and those who have struggled to learn,

for those who must keep love within easy reach
and those who can love across oceans,
for those who have ironclad rules about love
and those who have whimsical notions,

for those to whom love is a holiday treat,
a nice place to spend a vacation,
and those to whom love is a full-time career,
a twenty-four hour occupation,

for those who are miserly hoarders of love
and those who can never say no,
who fling it through windows and bounce it off walls
and give it wherever they go,

for those who are fully acquainted with love
and dine every night at its table,
for those who are ignorant failures at love
and fear they will never be able.

For all of us lovers, — and all of us are,
whatever our foibles or strengths,
let's love to the limit and even beyond,
let's go to inordinate lengths.
Let's love and let love be our glue and our guide,
let love be our choice and selection.
If we let love connect us, then love will direct us
and love us along to perfection.

Charlene

Charlene has a beautiful, firm body
with smooth, flawless skin,
a flat stomach,
and elegant legs
that are longer than the line-up
at the bank
on payday.
I love her.

Charlene has an understanding and devoted husband
who protects her,
when she so desires,
from the unending procession of young men
who long to drop to their knees and embrace,
for starters,
those superlative legs.
I love her.

Charlene has a newly-decorated home
in the country,
on a lake clean enough for swimming,
where city traffic never muffles the finch's songs
and there are no threats to be locked out.
I love her.

Charlene has an IQ of three hundred and fifty,
a mind which grasps
the essential nature of everything
and an unfettered intuition
which leaps to prophetic conclusions.
I love her.

Charlene has a job
that is challenging, satisfying,
and pays her exorbitantly
to do what she loves,
while prospective employers
plead to compensate her excessively
for just a twinkling of her time.
I love her.

Charlene has a talent for poetry
that gives her work
the power of a gospel,
the humour of the fearless.
the honesty of one who has no need
to be pretentious.
Audiences give her the accolade of a gasp,
a moment's silence before an ovation.
Poets reward her with acknowledged envy.
I hate the bitch.

Longevity, levity and brevity

On receiving a government cheque for $156.47

I feel it incumbent on me to mention
that I've qualified for my Canada Pension
but I'm not moanin' and I'm not grievin'
'cause gettin' old is gettin' even.

Sizing up

I have reached the age of wisdom
and we all know what that means, —
I am no longer willing to hold my breath
in order to do up my jeans.

The argument against eating potato chips in bed

I get crumbs and pieces
in my folds and creases.

Wimp in wolf's clothing

Well, I met this man
at a party last night
and he had an interesting kind of face,
craggy and weatherbeaten
and intriguingly lupine,
and an intelligent manner of expression
which I deemed worthy of exploration.
So I seated myself opposite him
on the porch rail and,
sipping the obligatory glass of white wine,
insinuated myself into the conversation.
We spoke of male/female matters
and I was at my scintillating best
in the thrust and parry of adversarial pretence,
with clever puns,
witty ripostes
and sparkling repartee
until, suddenly, he rose and stomped off,
muttering something about
aggressive bitch
and
feminist rhetoric.
I was taken aback,
amazed,
flabbergasted.
I had considered it foreplay.

Five second fantasy

His auburn hair —
waist-length, like my own,
ignited a spark of lust
in my tinder heart.
I envisioned us
tangled together
right there on the grass,
interwoven
in love's emulsifying art.
But then
I pictured the outraged neighbors,
forced to throw pails of conditioner on us,
to get us apart.

Viewing instructions

The winds that buffet and strip your banner
    rose far away,
        she said.
The fire that devours the bulwarks of your fortress
    is an impersonal flame.
The waves that rage and batter your harbour
    roll from ancient seas.
The earth that shakes and trembles your foundation
    shook and trembled long before you came.
Stand back and look once more at guilt
        she said
and re-examine shame.
There is no fault, no punishment,
no censure and no blame.
Sometimes,
        she said,
stones hurled by angry gods
and showers of unpolished gems
appear, at first, the same.

Cold comfort

When I'm flat on my back, looking up at the sky,
with a tear in my pants and a tear in my eye,
the last thing I need is for you to come by
and tell me it might have been worse.

When all my defences have seen fit to fail me
and worries and doubts and terrors assail me,
don't feel it your duty to heartily hail me
insisting it might have been worse.

When keen-edged injustice has cut to the quick
and the shit flung by fortune has started to stick,
don't offer, like some sanctimonious prick,
the theory it might have been worse.

When I'm in the clutches of doom and despair
over matters of health, or the heart, I don't care
to be comforted, soothed or consoled. Don't you dare,
as they're coming for me with the hearse,
to tell me it might have been worse.

Fish and company

My mother's hospitality's been legend all her life
and my father as a host was second only to his wife
but some things are not inherited so, love them as I may,
I tell my friends the rules of the house
whenever they come to stay.

You're welcome here three days as a guest,
if you want to stay for more
you've got to vacuum and dust and do the dishes
and mop the kitchen floor.
If you're thinking of staying as long as a week,
I feel obliged to mention
that the oven's due for cleaning
and the bathroom needs attention.
If you'd hoped to stay eight days or more,
I'm sure you wouldn't mind
some window washing,
and the carpet needs shampooing,
if you'd be so kind.
A ten days' stay calls for shopping and cooking
and polishing the silverware
and a bit of roofing and some plumbing work
and the odd electrical repair.

If you've got to be going, it's been good to see you.
I always enjoy your stays.
When they're short, they're sweet.
Come back next year
and you're welcome to stay three days.

Too late

Too late to be somebody else
too late to gather moss
too late to seek possessions
too late to mourn their loss

too late to pick another life
or chase a different dream
too late to hold my horses
or change them in midstream

too late for neglecting sunsets
or the night sky's shimmering jewels
too late for harboring grudges
or suffering deliberate fools

too late to rocket to success
too late to change my fashion
but way too late to settle for less
too late to cool the passion

too late by far for casual sex
and safe indiscriminate bedding
too late for lengthy engagements
and too late to wear white at my wedding

much much too late for early to bed
and too late for early to rise
too late to retract what should not have been said
too late for a word to the wise

when the ship has foundered on the rocks
too late to light the beacon
too late to save for a rainy day
when the roof's already leakin'

too late too late for holding back
for leaving songs unsung
too late to take a stitch in time
too late for dying young

too late for immortality
in this decaying form
too late for this anomaly
to set out to conform

too late to attempt to extinguish joy
to believe the dreadful news
too late to kick my boots off
to squeeze into high-heeled shoes

too late for fame or infamy
too late to gain or lose
too late for anything but love
to show me how to choose

too late to want to act my age
what would I do for kicks?
too late to shed old habits
too late to learn new tricks

too late to accede to someday
for heaven to be had
to compromise what's on my plate
too little?
    too late?
        too bad.

So far

Well, I'm sixty and I've hit my stride,
I've gained my soul and I've lost my pride.
Now there's nothing to lose and nothing to hide,
    so far.

Boogied on my birthday at the Cafe May,
the love was flowing every which way.
Seems to me like we're doing okay
    so far.

I'm the same age as Elizabeth Taylor
so Hi there, honey, and Hey there, sailor,
'cause she sure hasn't let sixty derail her
    so far.

I treat my body with respect,
well maybe a little benign neglect.
It serves as well as I protect,
    so far.

If you want to listen, I'll tell you the truth, -
sixty isn't the fountain of youth;
I'm long in the tits and long in the tooth
    so far.

Life is suffering and life is pain
and I'd rather not pass this way again,
but I'll laugh as long as I remain,
    so far.

Life and I, we've made a pact,
we're getting along just fine. In fact,
I'm not even trying to clean up my act
    so far.

The memory leaves a lot to chance
but the heart's still harboring romance
and the feet just want to get up and dance,
      so far.

I'm on the go and I'm in my prime.
I may start slow but I can stop on a dime
and it feels so good when I take my time,
      so far.

There are no limits to how we can grow.
If the mind is clear, it will tell us so.
Ignore the doubts that say you just go
      so far.

There aren't so many things I could
but there are fewer that I should
so it's all to the good. So far so good.
      So far.

Sweet revenge

She's probably left him by now.
He won't be the handsomest of men
or the sexiest, as he was back then.
It was bound to come, I just don't know when,
but she will have left him by now,

or maybe he's left her by now.
She's sure to have gotten wrinkled and plain
and that's certain to go against his grain
'cause he didn't desert me for her brain.
So I bet that he's left her by now.

Or, better yet, they're together, I hope,
and she's bored and cranky from trying to cope
with his aging prostate and his arthritis,
his heartburn and his gingivitis
and all the problems that assail
the failing frame of the older male.
And I'm sure she's tired and sick to tears
of having to live with, over the years,
the rattling noise his breathing makes
and the host of assorted pains and aches
he feels in his joints at a change in the weather.
Oh God, I hope they're still together.

Parting gift

I have seen the face of death
and held its hand
and kissed its brow.
I do not fear it now
or hate it.
While it may choose
to take from me
what I am loath to lose,
I find in it no malice.
Though it has drained
the body's bright ambrosia,
leaving me an empty chalice,
I know the spirit is not lost
but freed,
serving
as the sacrificial libation
of liberation.
And sometimes
death is what we need.

Retirement plan

When I am ancient — in a year or two,
and they figure I'm only fit for glue,
I'll have had the time to think it through
and I'll do some things I've been waiting to do.
I'll be finicky, crotchety and crabby
and I'll sit in the sun with an old grey tabby
and a chubby chihuahua on my lap
and I'll give no quarter and I'll take no crap.
And I'll pull no punches and I won't be kind
if it dulls the edge of my yataghan mind
which I'll subdivide with my rapier wit
and I'll give everybody a piece of it,
tactless and indiscreet, albeit —
the truth according to how I see it,
with instructions on how the world should be run
and almost everything ought to be done.
And no one will ever dare talk back
for fear it might give me a heart attack.
But I'll be a wise and a tough old bird
with a stubborn insistence on being heard
and I'll stay around until I'm finished
with all my faculties undiminished
and my eyes will be clear and my hands will be steady
and I'll die when I'm damn well good and ready.

Incensed

Not often, but from time to time, I wear
a scent that disappears upon the air
offering, in past or present tense,
no whisper of intrusion or offence.
I favour something subtle and discreet,
spicy and sensuous, while not too sweet,
a hint of passion, fragile as a flower,
to tempt or tease, but never overpower.
And all the women that I have presumed
to sniff are, likewise, sparingly perfumed.

But, oh my god, what's happened to the men?
They smelled so good all by themselves, and then
some hucksters launched a scurrilous assault
against male odors, — said men were at fault
and to be deemed effete and less than husky
if they were not both redolent and musky.
Men were malodorous, these hawkers told them,
and by the gallon and the ton they sold them
toiletries, soaps, pomades and aftershaves
that waft from them in overwhelming waves
and cling like cat spray. Polecat-like they reek.
One hug and you will bear their stink a week.
A chance encounter in an elevator
will leave your nose in shock till three days later.

Oh, for the fragrance of old-fashioned sweat,
of pheremones seductive and well met
or, failing that, a masculine cologne
that dissipates as quickly as my own
so one touch will not brand me, seasons hence,
like tree trunk, hydrant, pole or picket fence.

Take heed, young man, before you come to call,
smell like a man, or do not smell at all.

A consumer surveys

Tonight,
in case you hadn't noticed,
I am wearing a brand new, 100% cotton, plaid shirt.
It was an impulsive purchase
but, what the hell, it was on sale at Zellers
and I get a seniors' discount
which offsets the sales tax
and the occasional bargain is good for the soul.

This is a socially conscious shirt,
free of compulsion, collusion, corruption and karma.
No animals were sacrificed to produce this garment,
unless, perhaps, the odd boll weevil who got caught in the gin.
It owes not one buttonhole to enslaved prisoners,
sweatshop immigrants
or child labour,
having been manufactured, I am sure,
by happy, well-paid workers,
supervised by benevolent management
and shepherded by altruistic union representatives.
It was made,
according to the bilingual label,
in Moldova,
a Rumanian province which I picture to be high in literacy,
and low in unrest,
populated by a serene and industrious middle class
who love their jobs, their neighbours
and their democratically elected members of parliament.

I am, I realize, somewhat naive.
But I am aware of a number of life's bitter truths.
Gentlemen, I know, are not always gentle;
the Humane Society is sometimes less than humane
and women's liberation is an ironic oxymoron.
I trust, therefore, that I am not mistaken
in my assessment of Moldova,
lest my shirt end up
alongside my furlined coat,
my crocodile belt,
my deerskin vest,
my ivory earrings
and my wheel of French Brie
in my politically incorrect closet.

With a little more help

My life's been a shambles
of briars and brambles,
a chaos of shadowy fears;
my past was abysmal,
my future is dismal
with prospects of tortures and tears.

And that's how it goeth,
my cup underfloweth,
I look at my plate with distaste.
The blues and the greys
discolor my days;
it all seems a terrible waste.

But fortune arranges
transitions and changes
and little is ever for sure
so, when sick with despair,
I am always aware
that laughter and love are the cure.

And I gather with friends
to examine the trends
of our destinies' twisting and turning.
We talk at great length
of discovering strength
and the powerful lessons we're learning

from making our errors
and facing our terrors
and trials a day at a time,
no final solution,
just slow evolution
transcending the grim and the grime.

We tell and we share
and we love and we care
and we laugh with relief and release
and we speak about how
we're exploring the now
as the centre of power and peace.

We've learned how to cope,
with humour and hope
when we're feeling despondent and rotten.
I trust that, when next
I am troubled and vexed
and tested, I haven't forgotten.

Future imperfect

Despite my present miseries
I know, since everything decays,
that years from now, in retrospect,
these will be the good old days.

Winner take all

Nothing has changed
and nothing will change
and there is nothing to be done.
I cannot even formulate a wish,
not a solitary, lonely one,
that does not circle back upon itself
in an endless eddy of futility.

Time has not healed or dimmed or soothed
or softened with tranquillity
or sweetened with satisfaction
or righteousness
the bitter but inevitable action
that taints the flavour of my memory,
blighting the seeds of hope and laughter.

Regret is the ever after
of my side of the story.

I only wanted to see you happy.

You wanted to see me sorry.

For heaven's sake

For the love of me,
I can do little
to ease the suffering
of this world,
grown harsh and brittle.
But,
knowing that all life is one,
interdependent,
I strive with diligence
toward the mind transcendent.
For the love of all,
I take this aspiration,
I will stand helpless
in the face of pain
and seek purification.
And this is all,
for the love of me,
for the love of you,
with the greatest compassion,
I can do.

Reunion

During your visit
I was well behaved,
warm,
but not effusive
nor silly, as in the giddy past,
glad for the little friendship
we had saved
from the ash of passion
that once raged
too furiously to last.

We were both civil and civilized,
we made no mention of emotions.
Confidences were not invited,
dignity was maintained
and a wan shadow of the wit
we had so prized.
We did not touch.
No sparks were reignited.
We did not speak of loneliness
or pain
or mourning
for a precious, tender something
that had died.

And when you left,
and I could put pretense aside,
I sank below the brittle surface of my pride
and laid me down, exhausted,
between your cold and empty sheets
and cried.

Owned and unowned

I watched how my ego got caught on a poem
    — I hadn't imagined it would.
I thought, when I'd finished it,
    Does it connect?
and then
    Does it make me look good?

If that's how the ego had to act,
I'm glad it happened after the fact.

No position

Since I am rarely noticed lately,
except by panhandlers and pigeons,
I had decided that,
lacking attractiveness,
I would take pride in my invisibility.
So, yesterday afternoon,
I confidently strutted
my transparent splendour
through the oblivious throngs
on Yonge St.
But,
suddenly,
this total stranger came up to me,
asked the time
and inquired if I would like to go for a beer.
I blurted a startled refusal
and strode away from there,
noticing
that some days
the ego just can't find a place
to get comfortable.

All for the best

It's all for the best, they always say
and I've always tried to think that way
but I guess this just is not my day
because all for the best ain't great.

No, all for the best ain't all that good
and perhaps I may have misunderstood
'cause I've done the very best I could
and all for the best ain't great.

In spite of the leaps of faith I've leapt
and the stiff upper lip I've always kept,
there are too many painful tears I've wept
because all for the best ain't great.

I'd like to be an optimist,
someone that Lady Luck has kissed,
but all I get is a slap on the wrist
and a kick in the teeth, and I'm pretty pissed
'cause benevolence does not dictate
the vicissitudes of implacable fate
and all for the best ain't great.

Self centred

Through my ears, my eyes, my fingertips,
creation comes to know itself.
Over my lips,
as I remember to allow,
pass the milk and honey
of the here and now
and, drunk with fragrance,
I permit my nose
another toast
from nature to the rose.
All my experiences
I translate for all.
One crimson leaf tells,
to the oneness,
fall.
A glimpse of rusty breast
and grey-brown wing
speaks to totality,
through me,
of spring.
I am the conduit
for pain and bliss,
for laughter and despair
and anywhere I go,
aware,
all consciousness is there.
My every thought and each sensation
flows from the source and learns
through observation and through exploration
and to the source returns
singing itself in celebration.

I am a sentient cell,
common as all being
and, as all, unique.
I bear, within, the union that I seek
and share my sometimes seeing,
saying
there is no separation.
This vast entirety
is nothing more or less than love
dancing omnificent, omnipotent vibration
and you and I move and commune
within the whole,
centres of self-knowing
of the universal soul.

About the Author

Linda was born in Huntsville, Ontario, and was educated in Georgetown and Toronto. She lived for many years in Thunder Bay where she began the exploration of her evolution. As a result, she has become an active participant, rather than an impotent bystander, to the process which Carl Sagan describes as "matter coming to consciousness". She has two children who are almost as old as she is.

Linda returned to Toronto in 1978, working in a series of odd jobs until forced by friends to come out of the closet with her poetry in 1982. Now impossible to repress, Linda loves to give readings anywhere, anytime. As a member of *Uncritical Mass*, an ebullient trio of poets, she does so with gratifying frequency.

Her first book, ***Reflections From a Dusty Mirror***, was published in February, 1983. Once enough copies of it were sold to make room in her closet, she proceeded with indecorous haste to publish her second collection, ***What Do You Feed a Unicorn? Yesterday's Poetry*** was released in September of 1984 and ***It Was True at The Time*** appeared in October, 1988. Her most recent solo offering, ***Insights and Outlooks***, was published in November, 1991. ***Uncritical Mass in Consort***, a collaboration of love, was launched in 1995.

Linda's hobbies are poetry, eavesdropping, people watching and water. Her disciplines are beachcombing, brainpicking and breathwatching.

Printed in the USA
CPSIA information can be obtained
at www.ICGtesting.com
JSHW082223140824
68134JS00015B/712